LAND OF THE FREE

THE RIGHT TO VOTE

By
Elaine Pascoe

THE MILLBROOK PRESS
Brookfield, Connecticut

Published by The Millbrook Press, Inc.
2 Old New Milford Road
Brookfield, CT 06804
© 1997 Blackbirch Graphics, Inc.

5 4 3 2 1

Created and produced in association with Blackbirch Graphics.
Series Editor: Tanya Lee Stone
Editor: Lisa Clyde Nielsen
Associate Editor: Elizabeth M. Taylor
Production Editor: Laura Specht Patchkofsky

Photo credits
Cover and pages 6, 26: Photodisk; p. 5: Blackbirch Press, Inc.; p. 8: ©Cynthia
Johnson/Gamma Liaison; p. 9: ©Ralf-Finn Hestoft/SABA; p. 11:
©Ferry/Liaison USA; p. 14: ©Carol Halebian/Gamma Liaison; pp. 16, 21,
25: Library of Congress; p. 18: North Wind Picture Archives; p. 24: National
Portrait Gallery; pp. 31, 32, 33, 35, 39 (bottom), 41, 43: AP/Wide World
Photos; p. 34: ©Wright/Liaison USA; pp. 36, 39 (top left): ©Mark
Peterson/SABA; p. 39 (top right): ©Jim Bourg/Gamma Liaison; p. 42: ©Joel
Stettenheim/SABA.

Library of Congress Cataloging-in-Publication Data

Pascoe, Elaine.
The right to vote / Elaine Pascoe.
p. cm. — (Land of the free)
Includes bibliographical references and index.
Summary: Explores the basic right to vote for government
officials as it is guaranteed in the Bill of Rights, highlighting
the various restraints that were put on African Americans and
women in the past.
ISBN 0-7613-0066-X (lib. ed.)
1. Suffrage—United States—Juvenile literature. [1. Suffrage.]
I. Title. II. Series: Land of the free (Brookfield, Conn.)
JK1846.P37 1997
324.6'2'0973—dc20
96-21965 CIP AC

Contents

★ ★ ★ ★ ★ ★

Introduction

★ ★ ★ ★ ★ ★ ★ ★ ★ ★

Suppose that you could be arrested for reading a book, going to church, or talking with your friends. Sound impossible? Not everywhere. Your rights to do all these things, and many others, are guaranteed under U.S. law. But people in many other countries have no such guarantees. Their governments tell them what they may and may not read, write, and say, what religion they must follow, and even how they should vote—that is, if they are allowed to vote at all.

Americans are proud of their freedoms. Even so, many Americans don't know very much about those freedoms, or about the responsibilities that come with them. It is important to understand your rights, so that you can use them—and defend them.

The books in the *Land of the Free* series tell you about our most important American rights and freedoms: the right to speak freely, to vote in elections, to worship as we choose, and to join with others who share our views and goals. Most of these rights are set out in the U.S. Constitution and its first ten amendments, the Bill of Rights.

The Constitution and the Bill of Rights were written more than 200 years ago, soon after the United States won its independence from Britain. The authors of the Constitution believed that freedom would flourish under democracy. A democratic government, elected by the people, serves the people—not the other way around. Many of the rights in the Constitution help guarantee that democracy will continue.

The authors of the Constitution broke new ground, creating a society that valued and respected liberty. Over the years, adapting to changes in society, Americans have re-interpreted and expanded the rights that the country's founders set out. Yet, the basic principles behind those rights have not changed, and they apply just as well today as they did 200 years ago. Only if we understand how our freedoms work, and why they are essential, will they continue to flourish for years to come.

• The right to vote is considered the most important
right granted to citizens of a democracy.

Chapter 1

WHAT IS THE RIGHT TO VOTE?

When American citizens reach the age of 18, they can enjoy an essential right granted to them by the U.S. Constitution: the right to vote. This is one of the most important rights in a democracy—a nation governed by its people. Some people think that voting is the most important right of all. "The right to vote is the most basic right, without which all others are meaningless," American president Lyndon Johnson once said.

Why is voting so important? For one thing, Americans help to shape their country with their votes. They choose—or elect—their leaders, from the president of the United States all the way down to members of the local school board. They also vote to help decide the policies, or guiding principles, that will affect their daily lives. With their votes, they voice their opinions about how the country should be governed. Some issues are settled by voters directly. For example, should a city build a new elementary school? Voters decide.

The People Rule

Democracy springs from the idea that government should answer to the people, not the other way around. In a democracy, most government officials hold their jobs because they have been elected by the people. They have no hereditary rights to rule—that is, rights by birth—and they can't rule by force. When their terms end, they must run for re-election. If they lose the election they must leave office. Knowing that they must answer to voters keeps elected officials working toward what the people of a democratic nation want.

Leaders in a democracy rely on listening to and representing the voters who support them.

Direct Democracy and Representative Democracy

In the simplest form of democracy, people decide questions that affect the community by voting on them directly. This is direct democracy. Direct democracy dates back to ancient Greece. There, nearly 2,500 years ago, citizens met ten times a year in an assembly to decide important issues.

Direct democracy is practical only in small communities where there are fewer people, therefore fewer opinions to be considered. The work of city, state, and national government today is too great to be handled by direct democracy. The U.S. government, like nearly all democratic governments, is a representative democracy. In a representative democracy, people elect officials to represent them in government. Elected officials carry out the wishes of the people who voted them into office. On occasion, they may also need to do something that is unpopular—for example, raise taxes.

Something close to direct democracy survives in the United States today at the local

Individuals can voice their opinions at town meetings.

level, in what is called the New England town meeting. This meeting, a tradition that goes back to the Puritan days of the 1600s, is a gathering open to all citizens of the town. There, people discuss town business and vote on issues that affect them. But even towns that have this form of local government elect officials to carry on the day-to-day business of running their communities.

For a government to be truly democratic, all citizens must have the same basic rights and freedoms. People must be able to criticize government and express their ideas freely, without fear of being punished for doing so. And to reflect the wishes of the people, elections must be free and fair. That is, anyone meeting basic requirements, such as minimum age and citizenship, must be able to vote or to run for office; people must be able to cast (make) their votes in secret, without fearing that the government will punish them for making certain choices; and the votes must be accurately counted. When elections meet those tests, people truly benefit from their right to vote.

Americans enjoy the right to vote today, but it was not always so. As we'll see, it took many years for women and African Americans to gain the vote. Even after they had won the legal right to vote, African Americans were often prevented from doing so.

Who May Vote

The writers of the U.S. Constitution believed that all people must have a voice in their government, through the leaders they choose to represent them. The writers also believed that rules and procedures for voting, including the question of who should vote, should be largely decided by the states. Over the years, the Constitution was amended (changed) to prevent states from barring people from voting on the basis of race, sex, religion, or age. But the details of running elections were mostly left to state governments.

Today, even though each state sets its own voting requirements, most states generally follow the same guidelines. To vote, a citizen must be 18 or older and have lived in the state for a certain time. The length of this residency requirement is usually fairly short—six months or less. States do deny certain people the right to vote. For example, all states deny the right to vote to people who are not citizens of the United States and to imprisoned criminals.

Before voters cast their ballots, they must meet one other requirement: In all states except North Dakota, they must

Potential voters must meet certain requirements to register and be able to vote.

Kinds of Elections

The Constitution gave Congress the job of setting dates for presidential elections. States can, in theory, hold elections for other offices anytime—but they usually don't. Although presidential elections only occur every four years, other elections still fall on the same day a presidential election would. Election Day is the first Tuesday after the first Monday in November.

On Election Day, people may vote for candidates on the ballot (list) for any number of offices, from the president of the United States down to the town council. Here's a partial list:

National Government:
- President and vice president of the United States
- U.S. senator (member of the U.S. Senate)
- U.S. representative (member of the House of Representatives)

State Government:
- Governor and lieutenant governor
- Attorney general
- Comptroller (chief financial officer)
- Members of the state legislature
- State judges

Local Government:
- City and town mayors
- Members of county, city, and town councils
- District attorney
- Members of the local school board

register, or officially sign up. Towns and counties are divided into voting districts, and people register in the district where they live. At election time, registered voters can cast their ballots at their district's polling place. All a voter needs to do is present proof of age and residence in the state. States now allow voters to

- Sheriff
- Members of other local boards or commissions

Voters are also sometimes asked to decide important issues on Election Day. People may vote on a ballot question—for example, whether a state should change its constitution or pay for highway construction. In many states, citizens themselves can put such questions before voters. This is called a ballot initiative.

Election Day isn't the only time that voters go to the polls. Cities, towns, and sometimes states hold referendums. This is when people vote on specific issues—whether to build a new school, for example. A state may also call a special election to fill an office that becomes vacant before the next scheduled election. In addition, a recall election is something that may be held to decide whether to remove an elected official from office before his or her term ends. Recall elections are rare; they are generally called only when an official is accused of serious misconduct. And they rarely succeed. Most Americans feel that if a public official is doing a poor job, he or she can be voted out of office in the next election.

Most voters also take part in another type of election: a primary. In a primary election, held months before Election Day, voters go to the polls to choose their political party's candidates for office.

register through the mail, instead of appearing in person before a public official.

Most states have a registration deadline before each election. Voters who sign up after that date have to wait for the next election to vote. But some states allow people to register even on the day of the election itself.

Supporting a
political party
is one way in
which Americans
get involved in
the election
process.

Political Freedom

Along with the freedom to vote comes the freedom to take part in election campaigns, in which candidates (people who are running for office) try to convince the people to vote for them. For many Americans, taking part in a campaign includes supporting a political party. A political party is an organization that puts forward candidates for elected office. The party sets out a platform—a statement of its policies and principles—for voters to consider.

Besides naming candidates, political parties organize election campaigns, rallies, speeches, and debates between candidates. The Democratic party and the Republican party dominate American politics and government today. Other parties are small and do not have as much influence.

People are free to support any party or candidate they wish. This freedom goes hand in hand with the freedom to vote, and it's an essential part of the U.S. democratic system. When people register to vote, they are asked to express a party preference. There's no requirement to do so—voters can always register as independents, choosing no party.

Most people choose to register as Republicans or Democrats. When they do so, they can vote in their party's primaries. In most states, party members choose candidates in these primary elections. In a few states, though, parties choose candidates in caucuses, which are local meetings of party members.

Nothing in the Constitution requires the existence of political parties, but parties were formed in America soon after the Constitution was written in 1787. Now it is hard to imagine how elections could be held without them.

• Women called suffragists fought for many years to win their right to vote.
In 1920, they were finally granted that right.

Chapter 2

WINNING THE RIGHT TO VOTE

Americans fought the Revolutionary War to win independence from Great Britain and gain the right to govern themselves. To the leaders of the Revolution, "democracy" did not mean exactly the same thing that it means to us today. For example, in our nation's early days, only white men who owned property could vote. Today, all U.S. citizens over 18 can vote.

Why were so few people originally allowed to vote, and why did it take so long to extend the right to vote to all citizens? The answer lies partly in the view of democracy that came to America from Britain in colonial times.

Voting in Colonial America

The English colonists who arrived in North America in the 1600s governed themselves out of necessity. They had to find ways to keep order, defend themselves, and decide how their settlements would grow. They were better able to deal with these problems than the British king and Parliament, who were far away and occupied with affairs at home. For a while, Britain was content to let the colonies handle their own affairs.

Most colonies were governed by a governor and an assembly. In most cases, the governors were named by the British king, but some were chosen by the colonists. For example, John Winthrop, the first governor of Massachusetts Bay Colony, was elected by colonists. Members of the assemblies were elected by the colonists. The first of these assemblies, the Virginia House of Burgesses, met in 1619.

The American colonial assemblies copied many of their election traditions from those of the British House of Commons (part of the Parliament). In Britain, for instance, only men who owned property were allowed to vote or hold office. Similarly, the colonial

John Winthrop, the first governor of Massachusetts Bay Colony, was elected by the colonists.

governments set property ownership as a requirement for voting and for holding office. These restrictions varied from one American colony to the next. But every colony had a property requirement in order for its people to vote. Women, Native Americans, and African Americans were therefore excluded from the political process, because they generally did not own property.

As a result, in many colonies only a small number of leading families controlled the government. In Virginia during the 1750s, seven members of the wealthy Lee family served at the same time in the House of Burgesses. In Massachusetts, the children and grandchildren of the original Puritan settlers formed a core of political leaders who won election to the major colonial offices.

Since so many people were denied the right to vote, colonial elections did not truly represent the American people. They were not always fair, either—office seekers sometimes gave voters food, liquor, or even money to win their votes. Given its time in history, however, the colonial voting system was democratic. The idea that citizens should control their own government was still new—for centuries, European countries had been ruled by kings and queens.

Independence and Voting Rights

Colonial self-government was challenged as time went on. By the mid-1700s, the British tried to have more control over their colonies. They set new taxes and made other decisions that angered the settlers across the Atlantic. Since the colonists were not represented in the British Parliament, they had no voice in these actions. They fought the British government's decisions, saying "No taxation without representation."

In 1775, the American colonies revolted against Great Britain. Their main goal was to free themselves from the British government in order to form a government that would represent their wishes. In July 1776, representatives from the colonies met to create a groundbreaking document called the Declaration of Independence.

Most of the leaders of the American Revolution believed that people should control their government. They wanted a representative democracy—a government run by elected officials. Because they distrusted the power of kings, they favored the republican form of government, in which power is shared by an elected executive (president) and an elected legislature (a body of lawmakers).

Americans were also worried about giving too much power to a central government. Under the Articles of Confederation, the nation's first governing document, the thirteen states formed a loose union. The central government consisted of a Congress of delegates chosen by the states, and it was very weak. The states kept most powers, including the power to impose taxes, for themselves.

The state governments that were created after the Revolution had different rules about suffrage, or the right to vote. The Pennsylvania state constitution of 1776 abolished property ownership as a requirement for voting or holding office. All men who paid taxes were allowed to vote and hold office. Women, blacks, and Indians, however, were simply not given a voice in government.

Many of the state governments established in New England were influenced by the ideas of John Adams, a leader of the Revolution (who later became president). He was among those who feared that too much democracy might lead to "mob rule." He thought that state governors should have the right to veto, or reject, laws passed by legislatures. He also believed that both governors and state legislatures should be elected by the people—but only by those who had property.

The South Carolina state constitution of 1778 had some of the strictest property requirements for holding office. Candidates for governor could have no debts and had to own property worth at least 10,000 British pounds sterling ($450,000 in today's money). Anyone running for

The American Revolution was fought in order to allow the colonists to govern themselves.

the state assembly had to be worth at least 1,000 pounds ($45,000 today). These requirements meant that about 90 percent of South Carolina's white men could not run for office.

The New Jersey constitution established in 1776 gave the right to vote to all inhabitants who owned property worth 50 pounds ($2,000 today) or more. This wording allowed women who owned property to vote—and many did. By the early 1800s, though, men in power were worried that women were becoming too influential. In 1807, the New Jersey legislature withdrew women's right to vote. At the same time, New Jersey extended the vote to all white men, whether or not they owned property.

Extending Suffrage: Women and African Americans

In the early 1800s, the states gradually lowered and finally eliminated property requirements for voting. But generally, voting rights were still not extended to any group other than white men.

In 1848, Elizabeth Cady Stanton and Lucretia Mott—two leaders of a growing women's movement—called a convention, or meeting, in Seneca Falls, New York. Delegates to the meeting demanded equal rights for women, including the "sacred right to the franchise"—the right to vote. The Seneca Falls Convention was the first of a series of national women's rights conventions held annually through the 1850s. But women's efforts to win the vote made little progress in those years. And when the Civil War broke out in 1861, women put aside their efforts.

Alice Paul and the Fight for Voting Rights

The campaign to win voting rights for women had many leaders. But the one who captured the most public attention—and put the most pressure on government officials—was Alice Paul. Born in 1877, Paul first became involved in the women's rights movement in the early 1900s as a student in Great Britain. At that time, British women were also demanding voting rights. When Paul returned to the United States, she brought their protest tactics with her.

In 1913, Paul formed a new women's suffrage group. Eventually, it became known as the National Women's party. She and her followers organized protest marches. They protested at the White House and chained themselves to the fence—which was a shocking tactic for the time period. Paul was jailed three times for her protests. In jail, she staged a hunger strike, putting pressure on public officials by refusing to eat. She kept the issue of voting rights on the front pages of newspapers across the country. Her work helped win those rights for women.

Except in a few northern states, African Americans—whether slave or free—also had made little progress in winning the right to vote during America's early years. But with the end of the Civil War and the abolition of slavery in 1865, blacks prepared to enjoy the full benefits of citizenship, including the right to vote.

Members of Congress knew that many whites in the South would try to prevent the freed slaves from voting.

Thus, Congress passed the Fifteenth Amendment to the Constitution. Ratified (approved) by the states in 1870, it stated simply, "The right of citizens of the United States to vote shall not be denied or abridged by the United States or by any State on account of race, color, or previous condition of servitude." But, as we'll see in the next chapter, the amendment alone was not enough. Throughout the South, blacks were routinely denied what was now their constitutional right to vote.

When Congress voted to grant suffrage to freed slaves, many people expected that women would also

Lucretia Mott was one of the organizers of the Seneca Falls Convention, an important step in the women's rights movement.

win the right to vote. When this did not happen, women renewed their fight. They had their first success in 1869, when the territory of Wyoming allowed women to vote. They also managed to get a constitutional amendment introduced in Congress in 1878, but it did not pass.

The Nineteenth Amendment, which finally gave women the right to vote, was not ratified until 1920. The amendment passed in large part because of the important role that women played during World War I (1914–1918). Women took over the jobs that were left vacant by men who joined the army. Women served as nurses, raised money for the war effort, and did countless other things to serve their country. After that, most people felt that women could no longer be denied the right to vote.

This engraving celebrates the Fifteenth Amendment, which granted citizens the right to vote regardless of race.

• The Constitution provides for representation in the U.S. House of Representatives based on state population.

Chapter 3

PROTECTING THE RIGHT TO VOTE

Even after African Americans and women won the right to vote, there were serious inequalities in the American political system. In the 1960s, the U.S. Supreme Court heard some important court cases having to do with voting. In that same period, Congress passed laws to remove the obstacles that kept many blacks from voting.

Equal Representation

Under the Constitution, states are represented in the U.S. House of Representatives according to their population. The more people in a state, the more spots, or seats, that state has in the House.

The Electoral College

Every four years, American voters go to the polls to choose a president. But they don't elect the president directly. The U.S. Constitution set up an unusual system for presidential elections: the Electoral College. Under this system, the voters in each state choose a group of individuals called electors. The electors from all the states make up the Electoral College. In December, the electors meet and cast their ballots for the presidential candidates.

The results of the presidential election aren't official until the electoral vote (the votes of the electors) is in. However, everyone usually knows who the winner will be as soon as the popular vote (the votes cast by individuals) is counted. How can this be? When people go to the polls on Election Day in November to vote for the presidential candidate of their choice, they actually cast ballots for electors who have pledged to vote for that candidate in December. The winner of each state's popular vote wins all that state's electoral votes. The other candidates get none. Thus, the results of the popular vote allow people to predict the outcome of the electoral vote.

To become president, a candidate must win a majority of the electoral vote nationwide. Some people feel that this system is unfair because a candidate who loses the popular vote can still win a majority of the electoral vote. Here's how: A candidate may win a few big states by a narrow margin, gaining all their electoral votes. The opposing candidate may win more popular votes nationwide, but still end up with fewer electoral votes. This hasn't happened since 1888, when Grover Cleveland won the popular vote but lost the electoral vote to Benjamin Harrison, who had the electoral majority. Some people believe that the Electoral College should be abolished, and that presidents should be elected directly by popular vote.

Each state is broken into sections called congressional districts. The number of these districts a state has is equal to the number of representatives. Voters in each district elect one representative. In the same way, representatives to state legislatures are elected by voters in legislative districts.

In the late 1950s, Charles W. Baker and nine other voters in Tennessee went to court to challenge how the state's legislative districts were divided. According to Baker, the boundaries of the districts were unfairly drawn, giving more power to politicians in the countryside, and less to people who lived in cities.

For example, a rural district might have a population of 1,000 people and have one representative in the legislature. At the same time, a city district might have 100,000 people and still have only one representative. As a result, city people did not have the same degree of representation as rural people. A city representative spoke for ten times as many people as a rural representative, but the city representative still had only one vote in the state legislature. Thus city voters had less say in government than rural voters.

The case reached the U.S. Supreme Court as *Baker* v. *Carr*. In 1962, the Court ruled that states must draw legislative and congressional districts that are roughly balanced in population, to ensure equal representation. The ruling had far-reaching consequences. Most state legislatures had to redraw district lines to meet the "one man, one vote" requirement—that every voter have an equal voice in government.

Discrimination Against African Americans

In the early 1960s—almost 100 years after the abolition of slavery and the passage of the Fifteenth Amendment—African Americans throughout the South were still widely denied the right to vote. Many whites did not want African Americans to vote because whites wanted to keep political power.

This discrimination, or practice to keep power away from a minority group, was difficult to attack because the discrimination was not done directly. No state laws officially stated that African Americans were not allowed to vote. But many southern states had ways to keep blacks from voting. Some used the poll tax—a tax that had to be paid before a person could vote. Since many African Americans were poor, they could not afford to pay the tax.

African Americans were also kept away from the polls with literacy tests, which determine a person's ability to read or write. At this time, many African Americans did not have the same education as whites and many were not able to read. To exclude blacks, these tests were often made ridiculously difficult. For example, a black person wanting to register to vote might be asked to write a long essay on the meaning of the First Amendment to the Constitution. White people were simply excused from these tests and registered automatically.

Some whites also used violence to keep black people from voting. Some African Americans who tried to vote were beaten. Others had their homes burned. Fear of violence kept many blacks from even trying to register to vote.

Congress Acts

By the 1950s and 1960s, the civil rights movement in the United States was gaining strength. In this movement, African Americans challenged discrimination based on race. This movement had many important consequences. For example, the U.S. Supreme Court ruled in 1954 (in *Brown* v. *Board of Education of Topeka*) that segregated schools—separate schools for blacks and whites—were unconstitutional. Across the South, people challenged other kinds of racial segregation—on public buses, in restaurants and theaters, and in many other areas.

President Lyndon Johnson signed the landmark Voting Rights Act in 1965.

The 1965 Voting Rights Act

The 1965 Voting Rights Act established ways in which the federal government could get involved in a state and register voters who had been discriminated against. The law had four main points:

1. The federal government may intervene if fewer than half of eligible voters in a county or a state are registered to vote.
2. The federal government may suspend (temporarily stop) any tests or other devices used by the county or state to determine voter eligibility.
3. Federal examiners (people sent by the federal government) may then register qualified applicants to vote.
4. The federal government will continue to review progress in the county or state.

Nicholas Katzenbach

In 1965, Attorney General Nicholas Katzenbach used the act to end voter discrimination in the states of South Carolina, Alabama, Georgia, Louisiana, Mississippi, and Virginia; in 26 counties in North Carolina; and in one county in Arizona. South Carolina challenged the law in court, saying that it violated (went against) the constitutional separation of powers between the states and the federal government. In 1966, the Supreme Court ruled that the Voting Rights Act was constitutional in the case *South Carolina* v. *Katzenbach*.

At the same time, civil rights leaders worked to guarantee African Americans their right to vote. But action also had to come from the federal government. Eventually, it did. In 1964, the Twenty-fourth Amendment to the Constitution outlawed poll taxes. And in 1965, President Lyndon B. Johnson proposed the Voting Rights Act. This law allowed the federal government to keep states from discriminating against African Americans in elections. Congress quickly passed the law, bringing about huge changes, especially in the South.

Within a matter of years, hundreds of thousands of new voters registered. African-American candidates began to run for local offices such as mayor and sheriff—and they

By 1965, African Americans were granted true access to the American political system and began to register to vote in large numbers.

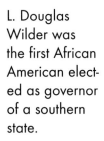

L. Douglas Wilder was the first African American elected as governor of a southern state.

won, which would have been unthinkable in the early 1960s. In 1965, only 100 blacks held office in the South. In 1989, by contrast, more than 3,000 blacks had held public office in southern states. Also in 1989, L. Douglas Wilder, an African American, was elected governor of Virginia. The fact that a black could be elected governor of a southern state showed the lasting power of the Voting Rights Act.

The Twenty-Sixth Amendment

From the earliest days, states had set 21 as the age at which people could first vote. There was a long tradition behind this age limit, going back centuries, to medieval times in England. There, under Anglo-Saxon law, 21 was the age at which people were considered to be adults.

By the 1960s, many people were urging that the voting age be lowered from 21 to 18. Eighteen-year-olds could serve in the military. People reasoned that if 18-year-olds could fight, and perhaps die, for their country, then they should certainly have a voice in government.

In 1971, the Twenty-sixth Amendment to the Constitution was ratified by the states. This amendment says, "The right of citizens of the United States, who are eighteen years of age, or older, to vote shall not be denied or abridged by the United States or by any state on account of age."

In 1971, the Twenty-sixth Amendment lowered the official voting age to 18.

At the time, some people worried that 18- to 21-year olds were not mature enough to vote. Young people, they said, might be easily influenced by political speeches or might vote for the "popular" candidate. But time has shown that young voters, like most people, think carefully about their votes before going into the voting booth.

• Exercising the right to vote honors the many Americans who have struggled and fought to win that right for all citizens.

Chapter 4

WHAT IT MEANS TO VOTE

As we've seen, Americans have struggled to get and keep the right to vote. Most Americans value that right. They put great thought and care into the choices they make on Election Day. Yet many people who are eligible to vote in the United States do not vote. Why is this so? And what does it mean for the future of the country?

An American Election

An election begins with a campaign. For weeks, sometimes months, before Election Day, candidates urge people to vote for them. They advertise, give speeches, even go door-to-door to shake voters' hands. And voters try to learn all they can about the candidates—who they are and where they stand on different issues. Voters also need to know about questions that may be appearing on the ballot.

How do voters get the information they need? Television news shows cover presidential campaigns and major state and city races.

(Running for office is sometimes referred to as "running a race.") Candidates often debate on television shortly before an election. These debates are a good way to learn how candidates feel about particular issues. Voters can often question candidates for local offices in person, at "meet-the-candidates" nights and similar events. Newspapers and magazines will print stories about the election campaign, the candidates, and the issues. These stories can go into greater depth than most television news shows can. Newspapers and magazines also print editorials—columns that express preferences for certain candidates or opinions on issues.

On Election Day, voters go to the polling place that is in their voting district. There, workers who are paid by the board of elections, or who are sometimes volunteers, check to make sure that people are registered to vote. Then each voter goes into a voting booth to cast his or her ballot in secret.

Some rural areas of the United States still use paper ballots, on which people write their choices by hand. Some cities have computerized ballots. But voters in most areas cast their ballots in mechanical voting machines. In these machines, the name of a candidate appears next to or under a lever or handle. The voter pulls the level next to the candidate's name. The vote is then recorded in the machine, which is locked.

When official voting hours are over, the workers from the board of elections record the total votes for each candidate. These totals are then reported to the board of elections. Depending on state law, absentee ballots—votes

Scenes from the presidential campaign of 1996:
Top left: President Clinton meets the voters in
New Hampshire; Top right: Pat Buchanan shakes
hands at a Republican rally; Bottom: Candidates
Phil Gramm (left) and Bob Dole (right) debate
the issues.

mailed in earlier by people who could not be present on Election Day—are counted by the board of elections and added to the total.

Why Do People Not Vote?

In 1988, more than 90 million Americans went to the polls to choose a new president. George Bush, the victor, won almost 49 million votes. The numbers sound huge—but, in fact, voter turnout was poor. More than 180 million Americans were qualified to vote in 1988, but only half of those who could vote actually did. Bush's 49 million votes represented just 27 percent of all those Americans who had the right to vote.

Voter turnout for presidential elections has fallen since 1960, when more than 62 percent of qualified voters cast their votes. The 1988 turnout was the lowest since 1924. In 1992, turnout rose slightly, to more than 55 percent. (In that year, three candidates ran for president, which helped to increase voter interest.) Even so, millions of people stayed home. And turnout in nonpresidential elections has been even lower. In 1994, just 38 percent of all those qualified voted.

Why do so many people not vote? There is no simple answer. Here are some of the reasons:

1. News coverage of campaigns has been criticized for being unhelpful. Critics say that newspapers, and especially television news shows, too often merely repeat catchy quotes from the candidates or discuss their personal lives. Many feel the media don't help people to understand the issues.

Increasing Voter Participation

How can people be encouraged to vote? One way is to get more people to register in the first place. For this reason, political parties and citizens' groups often sponsor voter registration drives in the months immediately before an election. States have made it easier to register, too. In many states, changes in registration procedures came as a result of the National Voter Registration Act, signed into law in 1993 by President Bill Clinton.

Known popularly as the "Motor Voter Law," this act requires states to allow citizens to register to vote when they apply for or renew their driver's license. It also requires states to let voters register by mail. And voter registration forms must be available in certain state agencies, such as welfare offices.

About half the states had mail or "motor voter" registration procedures before 1993. This new law guaranteed that these procedures would be available throughout the country.

Even people who register to vote may not actually go to the polls on Election Day. Some states, however, are finding ways to make it easier for people to vote. In Oregon, for example, voters were able to mail in ballots in a special election held to fill a U.S. Senate seat in 1996. It was the nation's first mail-in congressional election, and it was a great success—65 percent of registered voters cast ballots.

President Clinton signed the "Motor Voter Law" in 1993.

2. Many candidates run "negative" campaigns. That is, they run ads and give speeches criticizing and attacking their opponents. Negative campaigns can be effective—they often work. But opinion polls show that they also turn many voters off completely. In 1996, for example, presidential hopeful Steve Forbes lost the support of many voters by running a negative ad campaign.

3. Many people are discouraged and angry with their government and simply don't want to participate. Some feel that government hasn't done enough to solve serious social problems, such as crime. Others feel that government interferes too much in people's lives.

Around election time, many groups try to promote voter participation.

VOTER REGISTRATION

4. Many people think that politics is controlled more and more by special-interest groups such as business associations, labor unions, and many others. These groups pour money into election campaigns. Many people believe that elected officials will focus on those issues that these groups care about. The average person, they think, no longer has a voice in government.

There is some truth behind each of these views. But when people don't vote, they give up one of their most fundamental rights—as well as a chance to help solve the country's problems.

Getting involved in elections is one of the best ways young people can help to create a better country.

Voting Makes a Difference

In 1994, a U.S. congressman from Connecticut won re-election by only 13 votes. If just seven of those votes had gone to his opponent rather than to him, he would have lost. In the 1960 presidential election, John F. Kennedy won the popular vote by a little more than 100,000 votes. A few more votes in a couple of key states would have given a majority of the Electoral College vote to his opponent Richard Nixon.

Voting makes a difference. In the most basic way, votes determine which candidate wins. But votes also influence the policies that public officials follow after they're elected. When people go to the polls, they send politicians a message. The message may signal approval of the way an official has performed, or opposition to his or her views. Either way, voting is still the surest way to shape the society in which we live. It remains one of the most basic rights and most valuable freedoms of a democracy.

Understanding the Bill of Rights

★ ★

In 1791, the Bill of Rights became part of the U.S. Constitution. What are these rights and why are they important for us?

The First Amendment says that the government cannot interfere with people's rights to freedom of speech, freedom of the press, freedom of religion, and freedom of assembly. It also gives people the right to petition their leaders.

The Second Amendment says because a "well-regulated militia" is "necessary to the security of a free state," the government can't interfere with the people's right to "keep and bear arms." Arms are guns and other weapons.

At the time the Bill of Rights was written, most men still belonged to their local state militia, or army. They kept their guns at home so they could be ready to defend their country at a moment's notice.

Some people say that because we have no such state militia today, the Second Amendment doesn't give people the right to own guns. But other people say that the Second Amendment guarantees the right to own guns for many purposes, including defense of home and family.

The Third Amendment says that, except in time of war, troops cannot be lodged in private homes without the permission of homeowners. This was included because many people remembered a time when the British had forced citizens to open their homes to soldiers.

The Fourth Amendment says that people's homes and possessions can't be searched or taken without an official paper called a *warrant*. A warrant is a document, signed by a judge, that allows police to search for evidence of a crime. The amendment also says that a warrant cannot be issued without "*probable cause*." This means that the police must convince a judge that the search of a specific place is likely to produce evidence of a crime.

The Fifth Amendment protects people who are accused of crimes. It says that for a serious crime, such as murder, a person must be charged with the crime by a group called a grand jury. Twelve to twenty-three people make up a grand jury. They must examine the evidence that the government has against the person and then determine whether there is a strong enough case to charge the person with a crime.

The Fifth Amendment also says that a person can't be tried twice for the same crime and doesn't have to testify against himself or herself. In a trial, when someone who is on trial refuses to answer questions on the witness stand, we say the witness "takes the fifth."

Another important part of the Fifth Amendment says that no person can be "deprived of life, liberty, or property, without due process of law." This part of the amendment guarantees all citizens the right to a fair trial before they can be executed, put in prison, or have property taken away from them. It also means that any laws made in the United States must result in fair treatment of all citizens.

Last, the Fifth Amendment says that the government can't take anyone's property for public use without paying a fair price for it.

The Sixth Amendment gives people who are accused of crimes the right to a speedy and public trial by a jury of people from the area where the crime was committed. Without the right to a speedy trial, people could be arrested for crimes and stay in jail for years without ever having the chance to defend themselves in court. The amendment also says that those accused of crimes have the right to know their accusers, to be confronted by the people who have accused them, and to have a lawyer defend them.

The Seventh Amendment gives people involved in lawsuits over money or property the right to trial by a jury. It also says that once a decision is made by that jury, the decision can't be changed unless it can be shown that the trial was flawed in some way.

The Eighth Amendment protects people who are put in jail. The first part of the amendment says that a judge cannot require "excessive bail" for someone accused of a crime. Bail is money that a person must pay to be freed from jail during the time before a trial begins. The money is returned after a person shows up for trial.

The Eighth Amendment also says that no one can be given "cruel and unusual punishment" for a crime. If a person were convicted of stealing a loaf of bread, for example, it would be cruel and unusual punishment to sentence that person to ten years in jail. The rule against cruel and unusual punishment also prevents such things as the torture of prisoners.

The Ninth Amendment says that the fact that some rights are not specifically mentioned does not mean that the people do not have them.

The Tenth Amendment says that any powers not given to the government by the Constitution belong to the states and the people. This amendment was very important to people at the time the Bill of Rights was ratified. Many people still feared a large, powerful national government, and this amendment put limits on the government.

The Bill of Rights gave citizens of the United States many freedoms and protections that few people in other parts of the world had.

Glossary

★ ★ ★ ★ ★ ★

ballot initiative An issue or proposition placed on the ballot by citizens. Examples might include proposals to limit taxes or the term lengths of officials.

ballot question An issue or proposition placed on the ballot for voters to decide. Examples might include a change in a state constitution.

direct democracy A form of democracy in which people rule themselves, voting directly on issues rather than through representatives.

electoral vote The votes cast by members of the Electoral College in a presidential election.

literacy test A test that a citizen must pass before voting; once used to discriminate against African Americans

poll tax A tax that a citizen must pay before voting. Another means of discrimination, poll taxes were outlawed by a constitutional amendment.

popular vote The votes cast by individual voters in a presidential election.

primary An election that selects a political party's candidates for various positions in government.

recall election An election called to decide whether to remove an elected public official from office before the end of his or her term.

referendum A vote on a specific issue, such as a town budget or construction project.

register To sign up to vote.

representative democracy A form of democracy in which the people elect representatives to run the government.

residency requirement The length of time a person must live in a state before being permitted to vote there.

special election An election called to fill an office that becomes vacant before the next regularly scheduled election.

suffrage The right to vote.

town meeting A meeting, traditional in New England, at which townspeople vote on issues affecting the town. It is the closest thing to direct democracy in America today.

turnout The number of eligible voters who actually vote.

Further Reading

★ ★ ★ ★ ★ ★ ★ ★ ★ ★ ★

Brill, Marlene Targ. *Let Women Vote!* Brookfield, CT: The Millbrook Press, 1995.

Fradin, Dennis B. *Voting and Elections.* Chicago: Children's Press, 1985.

Samuels, Cynthia K. *It's a Free Country: A Young Person's Guide to Politics and Elections.* New York: Atheneum, 1988.

Scher, Linda. *The Vote: Making Your Voice Heard.* Austin, TX: Raintree Steck-Vaughn, 1993.

Smith, Betsy C. *Women Win the Vote.* Westwood, NJ: Silver Burdett Press, 1989.

Steins, Richard. *Our Elections.* Brookfield, CT: The Millbrook Press, 1994.

Index

★ ★ ★ ★